*This book is dedicated to my Mother
and Father who by their example taught
me the importance of giving and sharing.*

Greatful acknowledgment is given for permission
to quote from the following works:

Page 16 Reprinted by permission of Bantam Books,
a division of Bantam Doubleday Dell Publishing
Group, *The Light Beyond* by Raymond A. Moody, Jr.,
M.D., copyright © 1988 by Rayond A. Moody, Jr.

Page 17 Reprinted by permission of Benziger, a
division of Glencoe Publishing Co., *The New
American Bible*, copyright © 1970 by the
Confraternity of Christian Doctrine.

Author's note on pronoun usage: This book
contains numerous references to the third person
singular. Generally, whenever a pronoun refers to
both the masculine and the feminine, the plural
third personal pronoun will be used.

377
SIMPLE
WAYS YOU
CAN
MAKE A
DIFFERENCE

*Practical Suggestions For
Busy People*

MARIE ANGNARDO

HELPING HAND PUBLISHERS, CINCINNATI, OHIO

Copyright © 1994 by Marie Angnardo
Edited by Michael Lapmardo
Page layout by Robin Bedich
Cover by Sam Concialdi

Published in Cincinnati, Ohio by Helping Hand
Publishers, P.O. Box 58673, Cincinnati, Ohio 45258.

This book may be purchased in bulk at special discounts
when used as premiums, fund raising activities, sales
promotions, or educational purposes. For more
information, please contact the publisher.

Printed by Dickinson Press Inc., Grand Rapids, MI

Library of Congress Catalog Card Number: 94-75099

1994 1995 1996 HHP 10 9 8 7 6 5 4 3 2 1

Angnardo, Marie
377 Simple ways you can make a difference: practical
suggestions for busy people.

ISBN 0-9640406-0-3

For book trade ordering contact Login Publishers
Consortium, 1436 West Randolph Street,
Chicago, IL 60607, 1-800-626-4330

Printed in the United States of America

ACKNOWLEDGMENTS

I would like to express my sincere thanks to the many people who helped and encouraged me to complete this book: Jack York, Brian Krueger, Donna Capella, Michael Lapmardo, Robin Bedich, Neil Yutkin, Denise Bartick, Patty Burian, Rose Mulligan with Good Bears of the World, Michelle Cobey with Delta Society, Jackie Peckham with Guiding Eyes for the Blind, Pam Brown with *USA WEEKEND's* Make A Difference Day, Susan Knobler with LensCrafters, Linda Hellow with North American Riding for the Handicapped Association, Ruth Walters with Cincinnati County Jail Social Services, Andi Luketic with Heinz Baby Food, Ted Omohundro with Rotary International, Joyce Miller with Bethesda Corporate Communications, Mary Wright with Hospice of Cincinnati, Dick Schneider with the Non-Commissioned Officers Association, Nan Hankle Cecil with the Missing Children's Clearinghouse for Ohio, Fitz Core with SCORE, Gary Zocolo and Dominic Baragona with WN Broadcasting for the opportunity to work in community service during my years as Public Affairs Director, my brothers Tony Angnardo, Michael Angnardo, and Gerry Angnardo for their encouragement, and my dear Jim Wilson for loving me through the difficult times and always believing in me and this project.

Warning -Disclaimer

INTRODUCTION

One sentence in a book can affect you forever. It can make you stretch beyond what you thought you were capable of doing and see possibility in the impossible. One such sentence motivated me to look for ways busy people could make a difference - a challenge that seemed impossible at first. Before I share with you what that sentence was, I'd like to tell you more about this book.

Many of the suggestions in these pages are based on the recommendations of people who are already doing good works, charitable organizations that need help, business people who had ideas on improving relations with co-workers and customers, and ordinary people who commented on the small things that could be done to make them happier.

I spoke with a number of people who wanted to do more good things with their life but thought they lacked the time, energy, or money to do so. What I discovered was that many believed making a difference meant devoting long hours or large sums of money to a charitable group. They overlooked the possibilities for good a simple, single action could have.

Some of the ideas you will find here are quite basic such as calling someone if you're going to be late. It seems obvious, but haven't there been times when you've neglected to make that call? The problem was not that you were a bad person. Instead, you may not have been aware of the good results taking that action would have produced. Reading the suggestions in this book will sharpen your ability to recognize those opportunities and create some of your own.

GETTING MOTIVATED

Designing a life made up of good works takes time and effort. You must begin by developing your awareness and passion for doing good. Start by reading books and watching movies that inspire you to extend kindness to others. Charles Dickens' *A Christmas Carol* and Victor Hugo's *Les Miserables* are highly recommended. Attend lectures or seminars given by people who motivate you to be merciful. Keep a journal of the thoughtful things you see being done on television, in the news, at work, or wherever you are.

List on index cards the good works you've done and keep them in a recipe card file box. After you complete a good deed, write it on the front of the card. When you have moments of low self-esteem, lack confidence in your abilities, or question what you've done with your life, refer to your list. Discover how quickly you begin to feel good about yourself.

Give for the sheer pleasure of giving, and you will never be disappointed. Give because you *want to* give and not because you *have to* or because it's expected of you. Never look for repayment or gratitude, and you will always walk away from a good deed with pleasurable feelings no matter what response you get.

Don't be surprised, however, when your kindness and thoughtfulness are returned. They may not be from the person you've done a good deed for, but good things will start to happen in your life. Sometimes a good deed you do for one person may benefit another. How you treat someone can directly affect the way that person treats the next individual he encounters. Perhaps this explains why we experience unexpected kindnesses.

Recognize them when they occur. On the back of your index card where you've listed the good things you've done, list the good things that have happened to you. As you discover and experience the pleasures of doing good, you will want to do more. Eventually, doing good works will become a habit which comes naturally to you with little effort.

HOW TO BEGIN

Start by doing good deeds that are easy for you to perform then move onto those that require more effort. The following list outlines the **Seven Types of Good Works**. It is recommended that you perform your good deeds in this order at first. Do a few deeds in Type One until you feel comfortable moving to Type Two, Three, Four, etc.

Type One: Do something good for yourself. You must first feel good about who you are and what you have to offer before you can give to others. Recognize your self-worth and be good to yourself. Enroll in a class you've always wanted to take. Exercise. Read your favorite author's newest book. Look for opportunities to learn and grow. *Type One actions teach us we are worthy of good things.*

Type Two: Do something good for someone you love. It could be a parent, child, sibling, spouse, friend, or co-worker. Wash the car for your dad. Proofread a report for your co-worker. Take your wife out to dinner. *Type Two actions teach us how to get into the habit of doing good things for others rather than just ourselves. We learn how our little sacrifices may benefit others.*

Type Three: Do something good for someone you don't know. This is an action you extend to someone you don't know on a personal level. Generally, they're the people you pass by or hear about as you go on with your day. It's holding the elevator door open for someone. It's sending a teddy bear to a hospitalized child you read about in the paper. It's telling the woman who cleans your office what a terrific job she's doing. *Since most of us* *don't expect to encounter strangers again, Type Three actions teach us the pleasures of doing a good deed when repayment is not expected.*

Type Four: Do something good for someone who doesn't like you. These are people who for some reason just don't like you. They may not have said anything, but you know you rub them the wrong way. Usually, you don't have any ill feelings for them. Maybe there's another female co-worker in your office who can't stand you. On her birthday, give her a single rose to wish her well. *Type Four actions teach us the value of responding to negative feelings with good feelings.*

Type Five: Do something good for someone you don't like. These are people that you can't stand. Maybe they did something bad to you in the past, or you had an argument with them that hasn't been resolved. Call them and work out your differences. Invite them to dinner. Or, if you prefer to stay anonymous at first, send them a gift certificate to their favorite restaurant. *Type Five actions teach us how to put aside our ill thoughts and replace them with good ones.*

Type Six: Do something good for your community. You are now ready to perform a good deed that benefits many. The recipients of your kind or generous act are diverse. You many never know all who have benefited from your action. You could adopt a highway on Sundays and pick up the nearby litter. Arrange for your church choir to sing at a prison mass. Save your receipts from a grocery store that donates computers to local schools after a certain amount in receipts are collected. *Since these actions are usually done in cooperation with others, Type Six actions teach us how to work together to make good things happen. We also learn how one deed may affect many.*

Type Seven: Do something good for other living things. Do not neglect the needs of other living creatures. Take a half hour out of your busy day to play with your dog. Bring your pet to the veterinarian's office for a check up. Raise a puppy that will later be trained to help the visually or hearing impaired. *Type Seven actions teach us how to respect all forms of life.*

After you have completed a good deed in each of the categories, you should have a better understanding of the good you are capable of doing. Use the momentum you have built. Do at least one good deed a day. Schedule acts of kindness on your calendar.

THE IMPORTANCE OF DOING GOOD

Now, I would like to share with you the sentence that made me realize the importance of doing good. It is an observation Dr. Raymond A. Moody, Jr. uncovered in his study of near-death experiences. In his book, *The Light Beyond*,

Dr. Moody found that many people who were revived after being clinically dead had gone through the experience of being separated from their body, passing through a dark tunnel towards a bright light, and meeting a Being of Love who reviews their life with them.

During the life review, they see their actions but feel the affects their actions had on others. So, if a person as a child had taken candy away from a classmate at recess, he feels the deprivation and hurt the other child felt. The reverse is true as well. If he gave candy to a classmate who enjoyed the treat, he feels the same enjoyment the other child felt.

Dr. Moody wrote, "Through all of this, the Being is with those people, asking them what good they have done with their lives." (14).

Reading that sentence made me feel like a student who had just learned the question on the final exam from those who had taken the test earlier. What would I say when it was my turn to answer the question? What good had I done with my life?

Christians believe a teacher long ago revealed what would be on the final. Jesus said, "Come. You have my Father's blessing! Inherit the kingdom prepared for you from the creation of the world. For I was hungry and you gave me food, I was thirsty and you gave me drink. I was a stranger and you welcomed me, naked and you clothed me. I was ill and you comforted me, in prison and you came to visit me." (Mt. 25:34-36). Jesus revealed that whenever such acts of mercy were extended to another, it was done for him.

Whether or not you believe in the possibility of a life review, the benefits of doing good are quite clear. Many who have made an effort to do thoughtful things for others speak of having more self-esteem, better personal and business relationships, and a passion for living. Those who would like to start making a difference often don't know how to begin or what services are needed. That's where this book can help.

The suggestions on the following pages will help you recognize the many opportunities for good an ordinary day can bring. Right now, you could be calling someone you know who's lonely. You could be making sandwiches to drop off at a local food bank on your way to work. You could be giving recognition to a co-worker for a job well done.

Perhaps as you read this book, you'll come across a sentence that will show you how you can make a difference.

1

Bring your pet with you to a hospital or nursing home to help ease someone's loneliness. A visit could take only one hour out of your day. The Delta Society's Pet Partners Program offers training and instruction on how to become involved and can put you in contact with a facility that would welcome you and your pet. For more information, call the Delta Society at (800) 869-6898.

2

When it's somebody's birthday at work, distribute a card to all the employees and have them sign it with their own birthday message. This creates a sense of family at your workplace and makes the birthday person feel as though all remembered the special day.

3

After you've finished reading a newspaper in a public place, rather than throw it away, give it to someone who may want to read it.

4

Have your children and their friends make cards for hospitalized veterans during the holidays. The Non-Commissioned Officers Association of the United States (NCOA) sponsors Operation Appreciation during Christmas and Veterans Day. Mail the bundle of cards at least three weeks before the holiday to:

NCOA
225 N. Washington St.
Alexandria, VA. 22314

Cards from adults are also accepted. For more information call (703) 549-0311. Dick Schneider, National Director of State Veterans Affairs, says, "You should see the look on those veterans when they see the cards. They're just so happy to see them especially if they're from children."

5

Write someone else's name down when you mail in a rebate offer.

6

The next time you go through a fast food drive through, give the person handing you your food an unexpected tip.

7

Notify others when you're unable to keep an appointment.

8

Set up a program with your co-workers aimed at helping those in need. Collect a dollar once a month from all who wish to participate. Use the money to do something good.

9

Contact the principal of your local elementary school before the beginning of the school year. Find out if there is an underprivileged child who could use new school supplies. Fill a lunch box with crayons, glue, pencils, and scissors. Tie notebooks and paper to the bottom of the lunch box with a ribbon and drop off the materials at the principal's office.

10

Start a garden and give away the food you grow.

11

Purchase an audio cassette tape of Bill Cosby's stand-up routine and donate it to a hospice. Experts say hearing is the last sense to go, and studies find that humor helps ease the pain of illness. Find out if your local hospice maintains an audio cassette library for patients to borrow from.

12

Move up to the first gas pump.

13

Place flowers on a grave that doesn't have any.

14

Find out if your local school participates in Campbell's Labels for Education Program. If so, save the appropriate labels and give them to the school. The labels may be redeemed for various items including books, audio-visual aids, and playground equipment. For more information, call (800) 424-5331.

15

Make duplicates of photographs and give copies to people who are in them.

16

Show someone you appreciate the gift they gave you by using it in front of them. If it's a sweater, wear it. If it's a plant, water it. If it's a book, quote from it.

17

If you're an office manager, set aside at least one Friday a month as Casual Day. Some businesses allow employees to wear casual clothing every Friday. This practice does wonders for morale in the workplace and fosters a more comfortable working environment.

18

Hold a garage sale and donate the proceeds to charity. Not only will you clear out some of the items you no longer need, but you'll help a worthy cause.

19

Find out what surprises will make your spouse happy by trying this exercise. Each spouse should write down on strips of paper 10 things their spouse can do for them to show their love. Place his suggestions in one bag and hers in another. At the beginning of the week each spouse should pull one suggestion from the other's bag without saying what it is. During the week, surprise the other with the activity drawn. At the beginning of the following week, draw again.

Spouses may refuse to carry out an activity they do not feel comfortable with. If this occurs, simply ask your spouse to place a new suggestion in the bag. This exercise can bring spontaneity and romance in your relationship.

20

Invite someone to your gathering who's spending the holiday alone.

21

At your next party, invite guests to bring canned goods for "admission" and donate the items to a local food pantry.

22

Bake cookies or brownies and bring them to the office for people at work to enjoy.

23

If you rent a good video, ask neighbors if they'd like to see it before you have to take it back.

24

When you buy an upgrade of a computer software package, check and see if the software manufacturer participates in a school donation program. If the school qualifies, the software manufacturer may issue a new license to the school for your donated materials.

25

Return someone's call promptly.

26

Call an old high school friend you haven't spoken to for at least six months.

27

Attend a little league or softball game made up of children. After the game, go to the concession stand and have them deliver soft drink beverages to the losing team but don't tell the team you did it.

28

If you own a business and a customer has purchased a large amount of goods or services, tell them you're taking 10 percent off the bill because everybody could use a break now and then.

29

Leave a nice message on the answering machine of someone you know who lives alone. Call when they're away at work so when they get home they'll be surprised. Coming home to an empty place may not be pleasant, but seeing the message light on can make it a little less lonely.

30

Share you business expertise with someone who needs help in starting their own business. Contact your local Service Corps of Retired Executives (SCORE) office to see how you can assist the organization. SCORE is a program sponsored by the U.S. Small Business Administration which offers free counseling to prospective and existing business owners.

Experienced business people share their strategies at SCORE seminars for financing a business, keeping records, and increasing sales.

31

Have your co-workers pitch in to buy a dozen roses for a new employee on their first day at work. Place the roses on the employee's desk the night before with a card welcoming them to your company.

32

Set aside one day out of the week for family night. Let one person decide the evening's activities such as whether the family will go to the movies or play board games. The following week, let another family member do the choosing.

33

Contact the volunteer coordinator at your local hospital and offer to read stories to sick children. You could stop at the hospital once a week for a half hour and read to the children on your way home from work.

34

Buy gift certificates at a nearby movie theater for a family undergoing stress or hardship. This gift would be appropriate for a household struggling with unemployment or caring for a sick relative.

35

Give someone a free phone call. Allow a person to use your phone or calling card to talk with anyone they want for whatever time period you'd like to allot.

36

Call your local school district and find out if it has a call back program in which schools inform parents immediately if their child does not show up for class. The program is an effective way to protect a child's safety and to alert parents in the event a child is abducted.

37

Wake up an hour earlier on the weekend, and prepare a full breakfast for your family.

38

Buy a turkey from the grocery store and drop it off at your place of worship. Ask that the turkey be given to a needy family. This can be done during Thanksgiving or Christmas, but it's a bigger surprise when done outside the holiday season.

39

Write down all the special occasions you need to remember in your daily planner. Note all birthdays, anniversaries, holidays, weddings, and graduations. Make sure you acknowledge those important days with appropriate gifts, cards, and phone calls.

40

Warm up your spouse's car on a cold morning. Remove the snow and ice from the windows and keep the heater on. What a beautiful way to show your love by taking on the suffering your spouse would have had to endure.

41

Get in touch with a former teacher who's had a special influence on you. Tell them what they did that's stayed with you over the years and thank them.

For example, you can give the teacher who taught you how to enjoy reading, a hardcover copy of a children's book they read in class. Write a note on the inside cover saying this was the book that opened new worlds and ideas for you.

42

If you don't have a Christmas card list, prepare one today.

43

Review your Christmas card list. Select a friend you contact only once a year by way of a Christmas card. Rather than wait a full year for your next encounter, call your friend today and catch up on what's been happening.

44

Go to your place of worship and ask the priest, pastor, or rabbi what family is in need of financial assistance. Whatever the situation, give your church leader an envelope with money in it addressed to the family in need. You may want to include a note saying what the money is for. Have the church leader call the family and let them know that someone left an envelope for them. Ask that your identity remain a secret.

45

Always buy something when a child comes to your door selling raffle tickets or candy for fund raising projects.

46

Pray for someone tonight who's in need. It could be a woman you know who's going through a difficult time with her husband, a friend who's having stress at work, or a person you don't even know who's suffering.

47

Give someone a self-help book or tape that has made a difference in your life and will encourage others to discover their full potential.

48

Fast once a week so you'll know what it's like to be hungry. Use the money you save to feed those who don't have anything to eat.

49

Keep a container of aspirins or other over-the-counter painkillers in your drawer at work so you can offer them to a co-worker who has a headache.

50

Hire a young person in your neighborhood to cut your grass, rake leaves, or shovel your driveway.

51

If you know someone who wants to learn a new skill, help them take the first step. You could give them a brochure from a place that gives horseback riding lessons, a gift certificate for a computer training class, or a how-to book on gardening.

52

Put your shopping cart in the cart return area of the grocery store parking lot.

53

Talk with your children about the dangers of drug abuse. Arrange to have a former drug addict at a rehabilitation center discuss the affects of using drugs. Allow your children to learn from the experiences of others.

54

Order your Christmas or Hanukkah cards this year from the UNICEF catalog. Proceeds from your purchase will provide nutrition, health care, and education to impoverished children around the world.

Sending UNICEF cards also promotes the organization to others who may want to support its worthy causes. To order a UNICEF catalog, call (800) 553-1200.

55

Call and let a loved one know when you've arrived safely from a trip.

56

Prepare a big thermos of hot chocolate before going to a football game. Bring extra cups and offer some hot chocolate to those sitting near you. It's a delicious way to spread warmth to others.

57

Pay your debts on time. Others may be relying on your prompt payment.

58

Write a letter to a friend of yours whom you haven't been in contact with for more than a year.

59

At least once a day, exchange conversation with someone you haven't spoken to before. It doesn't have to be anything of great length. It could be a simple, "Good morning," to the person in the elevator.

60

Buy a plant for a person who can't leave their home due to illness or a disability. Some shut-ins feel so lonely and useless that caring for a plant makes them feel vibrant again. Ask an organization that serves the disabled in your area who might appreciate such a gift.

61

Take someone to a place where you've
discovered a beautiful view.

62

Collect the loose change from your
pockets or purse and place them in a jar.
When it's full, exchange the coins for
bills and use the money to do good things
for others.

63

If you haven't been to a religious service in a long time, go this weekend. If you don't feel like participating in full, then sit in the back and absorb the feelings and emotions you experience.

64

Show your customers how much you appreciate their business by offering them a chance to win a free service or product. Have customers place their business cards in a plastic container and draw a name weekly or monthly to award the free service or product.

65

Be patient when a salesperson, customer service representative, or food server is busy.

66

When you see a group of neighborhood kids gathered around an ice cream truck, treat them all to their favorite selection.

67

Save your old magazines and donate them to a nursing home, youth center, or prison. If you'd like to remain anonymous, remove the mailing label showing your name and address from the magazine.

68

Warm up a pair of thick socks by the heater for your loved ones to put on when they come in from a wet or snowy day.

69

Let someone else take a parking space you've been waiting for.

70

Read the newspaper and see who can use your help. Send money to a family that has a child who needs a bone marrow transplant, write a few words of encouragement to a student going to the state finals, and send clippings to parents whose child's accomplishments are featured in the article.

71

Offer to baby-sit for a couple you know who could use some time alone together.

72

Share your secret with an engaged couple for having a long and happy marriage.

73

Don't park in the handicapped space.

74

Walk a woman you know to her car at night.

75

Invite grade school students to your office to learn more about your profession.

76

Go through your closets and drawers. If you haven't worn an article of clothing for at least two years, put it in a pile. Wash or dry clean the clothes, and drop them off at Goodwill or the Salvation Army.

77

Give a co-worker who's having car trouble a ride to work.

78

Find out where someone is going to spend their vacation and surprise them with tickets to an event that is in the area. For example, if a couple is spending the weekend in New York City, have a pair of theater tickets waiting for them at the front desk of their hotel.

79

When you're running late for an appointment, notify the other party how late you'll be.

80

Buy someone a subscription to a magazine they're interested in, but don't tell them you did it.

81

Make someone in your household freshly squeezed orange juice.

82

Ask someone's permission before you take something of theirs.

83

Return what you borrow.

84

Kiss your spouse before leaving for work.

85

Call your sweetheart during the day at work just to say, "I love you."

86

When you've dialed the wrong number, apologize to the other party. Don't just hang up.

87

Find an area of your neighborhood that can be enhanced with more beauty. See what you can do to make it look better, and present your proposal to local officials if necessary. For example, if graffiti is covering a downtown wall, organize a group to paint over it one afternoon.

88

Invite someone to your house of worship who may not be practicing a particular faith.

89

Give information on employment opportunities to someone who's looking for a job.

90

Shovel the snow from an elderly person's driveway.

91

The next time someone asks you for something, give a little more than what they've asked for. For instance, if they ask you to baby-sit for two hours, offer to baby-sit for three hours.

92

Sign an organ donor card.

93

If you're fluent in a second language, teach it to your children when they're young.

94

Volunteer to work a few hours at a church festival booth.

95

Pick up or drive someone to the airport rather than have them take a taxi.

96

Wash and wax a family member's car and fill up the gas tank.

97

Make sure your family is well provided for in the event that something should happen to you. Get life insurance and make out a will.

98

Let someone else have the TV remote control.

99

Impulsively stop by a flower vendor's cart and buy your companion a flower.

100

Make a wish come true for children with a terminal or life threatening illness. Find out how you or your company can help children live their dreams. Call the Make-A-Wish Foundation for more information at (800) 722-WISH (9474).

Businesses can sponsor a wish by offsetting some of the cost of a wish or by donating their services. Volunteers are needed to help grant wishes, to organize special events, or assist in other ways. More than 23,000 wishes have been granted since 1980.

101

Offer to help your host clean up after a party.

102

Introduce yourself to your priest, pastor, or rabbi. Get to know your church leader in a social setting.

103

When talking with someone, use their name.

104

Provide clean bed sheets and towels for your house guests.

105

Engrave special gifts.

106

When it's your loved one's birthday, call their favorite radio station and ask the disc jockeys on the morning show to wish your loved one a happy birthday over the air.

107

When you're a passenger in a car with someone who needs gas, step out and pump the gas for them.

108

Send a care package to a young person you know who's away from home for the first time.

109

Place coins in a laundry mat machine with a note inviting someone to enjoy a free load of wash.

110

Pick up your candy wrappers, cups, and popcorn containers after watching a movie at a theater, and throw them away in the garbage can.

111

Make sure you aren't over the limit when you get into the express lane at the grocery store check out line.

112

Donate old books to your local public library and add to its collection. If the library cannot retain the books, it may decide to sell them as part of its fund raising activities. Many libraries conduct book sales to generate revenue.

113

Call before you stop by someone's house for a visit.

114

Always put money in the Salvation Army kettle during the Christmas season.

115

The following are good things you can do for others in your household:

Take good phone messages and deliver them promptly...

116

Fill the ice cube tray with water when you see that more than half of the ice cubes are gone...

117

Sweep the garage...

118

Vacuum the carpets in the house...

119

Do the laundry, fold, and put away the clothes...

120

Iron wrinkled clothes...

121

Prepare and cook meals...

122

Buy groceries or help bring in the groceries from the car if someone else in your household purchased them...

123

Wipe the table after meals...

124

Do the dishes and empty the dishwasher...

125

Dust and polish the furniture...

126

Leave room in the driveway for other cars to get in and out when you park...

127

Wipe your feet before entering the home...

128

Hang your towel on a rack rather than throw it on the floor or leave it on the counter...

129

Flush the toilet after using it...

130

Pick up the take out order from a restaurant...

131

Keep the volume on your stereo down...

132

Make home videos with household members...

133

Help place the decorations on the Christmas tree, and remove them after the holiday...

134

Hang up your clothes...

135

Make your bed in the morning, clean your room, and keep it neat...

136

Cut the grass...

137

Take out the garbage...

138

Rake the leaves in your yard...

139

Shovel the snow on your driveway, porch, and sidewalk...

140

Set the table before a meal...

141

If you live in a large household, conserve hot water for others while you take your shower...

142

Remove your hair from the tub after showering...

143

Wipe the bathroom floor if it's wet after showering...

144

Clean the inside of the refrigerator by throwing away spoiled food...

145

Replace a burned out light bulb...

146

Respect each other's privacy. Knock before you enter someone's room...

147

Wrap leftover food after a meal and place it in the refrigerator...

148

Scrub the tub and sink with a bathroom cleaner...

149

Clean the toilet bowl with a brush and toilet cleaner...

150

Make sure all the doors are locked before going to sleep...

151

Take care of the household pet by feeding it, playing with it, cleaning up after it, and bringing it to the veterinarian...

152

Eat at least one meal a week together with all members of your household...

153

Let someone else in your household use the bathroom before you do...

154

~~~

Replace an empty roll of toilet paper. Don't just leave one sheet for the next person...

155

~~~

Remove lint from the dryer after each load...

156

~~~

Leave the porch light on when someone in your household goes out at night...

157

Help guests unload their luggage from the car when they visit you...

158

Take rented videos back to the video store...

159

If you have the TV remote control, don't keep changing the channels when others are watching a program.

160

Help people accomplish their goals. If they want to watch all the movies nominated for the Best Picture Oscar, go with them to the theater. If they want to find out which restaurant in your city makes the best pizza, accompany them on the taste testing mission.

161

Mail coupons for baby related items to new parents.

162

Bring extra cotton with you to a concert. Offer some to those sitting next to you if the music's too loud to protect their hearing.

163

Don't let someone who's had too much to drink behind the wheel of a car. Drive them home, call a cab, or let them sleep at your place.

164

Call the police if you see a drunk driver swerving on the road. Get a description of the vehicle, license plate number, and direction in which it's going.

165

Make every effort to be on time.

166

Videotape a program for someone you know who may find it interesting.

167

Call the volunteer coordinator of a nearby nursing home, and find out how many patients reside at the facility. Arrange to have a helium-filled balloon delivered to each person. This may be done for any major holiday. It's especially touching if done on Valentine's Day.

168

Give someone an autographed book by a favorite author.

169

Learn how to perform basic first-aid procedures. Contact the American Red Cross in your area for more information on training classes.

170

Help others move into a new home.

171

Take an anonymous AIDS test. Find out from your county health department where such tests are given.

172

Teach your child how to call 911 in an emergency.

173

Travel a long distance just to see a friend or relative. Your action tells them that they're special to you and that you'd go out of your way for them.

174

Attend your child's school or athletic functions. All children want to make their parents proud of them. Give them your support with your presence.

175

Leave love notes for your spouse to find in various places like the driver's seat of a car, in the refrigerator, or on a pillow.

176

Tell a store manager when someone's left their car lights on in the parking lot.

177

Donate long, thermal underwear to inmates at your local jail during the winter months.

178

Volunteer to answer phones for an hour at a telethon you support.

179

Clean up your dog's mess after you walk him. Your neighbors will appreciate this action.

180

Gather friends together during the Christmas season, and sing carols at a nursing home. Make arrangements with officials at the facility first. Go into each room and ask each person what their favorite Christmas song is, and sing it. Give a candy cane to each person you visit.

As an added touch, bring children along to distribute the candy. Many elderly people enjoy seeing the faces of young children. This activity should take about one hour.

181

Check to see that all of your passengers are wearing their seatbelts before you drive off.

182

Make sure your car's turn signal is off after you've completed your turn. Driving for miles with a blinking turn signal can cause accidents.

183

Turn the bright lights of your car off when another vehicle is facing you. Keeping them on is a distraction to the other driver and limits their visibility.

184

Instead of selling or trading in your old car, donate it to a local church for a needy family.

185

When driving, signal before you turn.

186

When coaching a team of young children, let all of them play. Don't let anyone sit the bench for the entire game.

187

Patronize local businesses.

188

Take a cold pitcher of iced tea along with some tall glasses filled with ice to workers who have been laboring in the sun.

189

Rinse and save your soft drink beverage cans. Drop them off at a recycling center.

190

Attend a lecture given by a missionary or someone who has returned from the Peace Corps. You'll be reminded of how much more needs to be done to help the world's poor.

191

Invite a neighbor to your home for coffee and relaxing conversation.

192

Pledge money to a charity telethon you support. Your business may want to do a promotion that benefits the telethon.

193

Attend a friend's wedding.

194

Offer to be a reference for someone needing a recommendation for a job.

195

Let your passengers get out of the car before you park in a crowded lot or if it's raining or bitterly cold.

196

Always bring a covered dish, dessert, wine, or bag of chips to a party.

197

Find out if your local hospital needs volunteers to care for "boarder babies." Thousands of babies are abandoned in hospitals every year by mothers who have drug addictions or are HIV-positive. Volunteers visit "boarder babies" and give them the affection they crave by gently rocking them in the nursery.

198

During the first real snowfall of the season, make a snowman with your child.

199

Give relief to families who care for a person with chronic illness or disabilities. Help clean their house one afternoon, pick up a bag of groceries, or watch the person while the caregiver takes a much needed break.

200

Encourage employees to recognize the good works their co-workers are doing on the job. SARCOM Educational Services in Cincinnati, Ohio holds monthly meetings to update employees on company developments and to award "10 to 1" cards to deserving personnel.

Throughout the month, employees inform their manager when they think a co-worker deserves a "10 to 1" card for an extraordinarily good job performance, such as having a positive attitude under pressure. The manager decides whether the circumstances warrant an award. After an employee receives 10 cards, they may be traded in for a paid day off from work.

201

Spend a weekend with your spouse at a Marriage Encounter weekend.

202

Rent the movie *Magnificent Obsession* starring Jane Wyman and Rock Hudson. The movie, based on the novel by Lloyd C. Douglas, explores a man's commitment to a way of life in which he is of service to others, keeps his good deeds a secret, and refuses repayment from those he helps.

203

Hire someone who has a disability.

204

Arrange a field trip in the summer for young children in your neighborhood to learn new things. It could be a trip to the local museum, fire department, or TV station.

205

Let friends know your change of address and new phone number after your move.

206

Spend an hour picking up litter at a park or playground.

207

Let someone who has fewer items get in front of you at the check out line of the grocery store.

208

Always be faithful to your spouse.

209

Call and wish someone luck before a job interview.

210

Donate blood at your local American Red Cross chapter.

211

Take the time to wrap a gift. Don't just give someone a present in the same bag you got from the store.

212

Many schools, churches, clubs, and non-profit organizations conduct fund raising events centered around meals such as a pancake and sausage breakfast or fish fry. When you learn that such an event is being held near you, eat a meal at the function and support a worthy cause.

213

Send postcards to loved ones when away on a trip.

214

Always come back from a trip with gifts for loved ones.

215

Call the police when you see a stranded motorist on the highway. Let the police know the motorist's location by noting what exit the car is near.

216

Have your company buy a pair of season tickets to a popular professional sporting event in your city (baseball, baskeball, football, etc.). Invite employees to use the company tickets or offer them as incentives for excellent work.

217

Say you're sorry when an action you've taken has hurt someone. Do whatever is possible to correct the situation.

218

Offer to change work shifts or vacation days with someone who has special plans when you're scheduled to be off from work.

219

Pay your respects at a wake or funeral. Share a fond memory with the deceased's loved ones. Make it a memory that describes how the deceased did something good for another person.

220

Walk horses carrying disabled riders at a therapeutic riding center. It's a terrific opportunity for you to enjoy the outdoors, get some good walking exercise, and help a disabled person improve their skills.

Generally, a riding session lasts about one hour and benefits the rider physically, mentally, and emotionally. Prior experience with horses is required for volunteers who lead horses. However, no horse experience is required for other volunteer roles. For information on a therapeutic riding center near you, call North American Riding for the Handicapped Association in Denver, Colorado at (800) 369-RIDE (7433).

221

Comfort a child lost in a public place, and help locate the parents.

222

Write to public officials about an issue that concerns you. If a law needs to be changed, work with officials to get it done.

223

Buy a cold drink on a summer afternoon from enterprising children who have put up a lemonade stand in their front yard.

224

If you use a house bowling ball, return it to the rack after you've finished bowling. Don't just leave it on your lane.

225

Accompany someone if they plan to be out late alone at night.

226

When opening your car door, be careful not to hit the car parked next to you.

227

Donate your old eyeglasses to help underprivileged people in developing countries see more clearly. Give the Gift of Sight, co-sponsored by LensCrafters and Lions Clubs International, is a program in which donated eyeglasses are cleaned, repaired, classified by prescription, and distributed to visually impaired people in developing countries. Simply drop off the eyeglasses at your nearest LensCrafters store. Prescription and non-prescription sunglasses are also welcome. Call (800) 522-LENS (5367) for store locations.

228

Pick up scraps of paper you notice on the floor at home, at the office, or at a public place, and throw them away. Don't just walk by them. If there's any way you can leave a place a little cleaner or nicer, do it.

229

Change the battery in your home fire alarm.

230

If someone you know is hospitalized during a holiday, decorate their room accordingly to help them celebrate the special day.

231

〜〇〜

Participate in USA WEEKEND's Make A Difference Day which is a national day of volunteering held every fourth Saturday in October. Individuals, families, co-workers, and groups have performed such good deeds as winterizing houses, organizing food and clothing drives, and planting trees. Coordinators of the event encourage participants to continue their projects throughout the year. For more information on how you can take action, write:

USA WEEKEND MAKE A DIFFERENCE DAY
1000 WILSON BLVD.
ARLINGTON, VA. 22229-0012

Ten outstanding projects are each awarded $2,000 to benefit a worthy cause. Additionally, key participants attend an awards ceremony in Washington, D.C.

232

Become a host family in the Rotary International Youth Exchange Program. Host families allow foreign exchange students to live in their home as a member of the family to learn the country's culture and customs while attending school. Students live with host families for approximately three months before going to live with another host family. For more information, call your local Rotary club or the Rotary International office in Evanston, Illinois at (708) 866-3421.

233

Place a blanket over someone who has fallen asleep on your couch.

234

Become an active member of your church or synagogue. As long as you plan on attending the service, find out how you can be of assistance while there. Be a reader, an usher, take up the gifts, or distribute communion.

235

Frame pictures of loved ones, and hang them up so when they visit, they can see how important they are to you.

236

When giving someone a book as a gift, always write a brief note with the sentiments you feel about the person inscribed on the inside cover.

237

Attend Parent-Teacher Conference meetings to discuss your child's academic progress.

238

When older teenagers are left alone in the house for a few days because their parents are out of town, invite them to your home for dinner. Find out if they need anything.

239

Ask someone to do something, don't tell them.

240

Say "Good morning," to your co-workers when you first arrive at the office.

241

Display letters your company gets in the mail from customers commenting on the good products or services they received from your company and employees. Frame the letters, and place them in the reception area. Not only will your clients read about the quality work you provide, but your employees will feel valued as well. If the letter mentions a particular employee, give the employee a copy of the letter, praise them for doing a good job, and tell them you're placing a copy in their personnel file.

242

Keep your work area in the office neatly organized. Your co-workers may find it difficult or distracting to perform their jobs if your space is a mess especially if they have to refer to important files or reports on your desk. Always end the day with a clean desk.

243

Before you leave on vacation, make a list of the items your co-workers must handle, and review the information with them so they may ask you questions. Instruct them where to find pertinent information about an account or client who has pending needs.

244

Call your co-workers in the middle of your vacation if possible to see if they need any information from you.

245

Tell your clergyman after a religious service when they've given an excellent sermon.

246

When writing a card for someone, include the person's name in the card with the date to personalize it. Many people save cards and look through them years later. Seeing your name written in the handwriting of someone you love brings an added value to the card.

247

Bring flowers and a card to the office for your secretary on Secretaries Day.

248

Pay for the flight ticket for someone to spend the holiday with friends or family who might otherwise not be able to see them. Try to keep this gift a surprise.

249

Hold the elevator door open for someone who's running to catch it.

250

Install basketball nets on playground basketball hoops that don't have any. Many public basketball hoops have been stripped of their nets.

251

Teach someone how to dance.

252

Bring a housewarming gift to friends who have moved into a new house or apartment.

253

If driving conditions are poor in severe weather and threaten to get worse, allow your employees to go home early.

254

If your company's parking lot and sidewalks are slick and icy, arrange to have salt poured on the ground to avoid accidents.

255

Say "please" when requesting something from someone.

256

Smile at others. It will brighten their disposition and help you maintain a good mood. It's difficult to smile for any length of time and be depressed or upset.

257

Give the gift of laughter. Tell someone a funny joke you heard that may be shared with others.

258

During the cold season, keep a handful of cough drops in your purse or coat pocket. Offer them to others who have a bad cough.

259

Fill out comment cards when presented with them, and give your sincere observation of the company, service, or product. Whenever possible, include positive comments.

260

Write a letter to the manager or president of a company where you've received excellent service. Include names whenever possible.

261

Support the Mothers Against Drunk Driving message by participating in its National Red Ribbon Campaign from November through January. Tie a red ribbon to your car as a reminder to motorists of the dangers of drinking and driving especially during the holidays. Call your local MADD office for the ribbon or the national office at (800) GET-MADD (438-6233) for information on chapter locations.

262

When you hear a siren while driving, slow down and pull over to the side of the road to let the emergency vehicle pass. Say a small prayer for whomever may be in need.

263

Make cold cut sandwiches, and drop them off at a local soup kitchen on your way to work in the morning.

264

Help a needy family pay for their gas and electric bill. Call your local welfare office to find out which household is in danger of having their power turned off. Make arrangements with the gas and electric company in cooperation with the welfare office to pay the bill. This good deed may be performed without the recipient knowing your name.

265

Light a candle in church for someone's special intention.

266

Contribute to your local public television station during its membership drive. Your donation helps bring quality news, educational, and cultural programming to viewers in your community.

267

Sign a petition for an issue you feel strongly about.

268

Put harmful household items out of children's reach.

269

When making out your shopping list, include items for the poor. Rather than donate items that are leftover from your household, be conscious of the needy while shopping. Use coupons to help defray the cost. The following items are needed at various shelters for men, women, and children:

Socks, gloves, underwear, toilet paper, shampoo, feminine hygiene products, toothpaste, toothbrushes, shaving cream, razors, soap, disposable diapers, infant formula, baby wipes, deodorant, blankets, clothing, laundry detergent, and non-perishable foods such as canned fruits and vegetables, soup, tuna, pastas, powered milk, cereal, and canned meats. Donate these items at a shelter near you.

270

Write a thank you note to someone who has done something thoughtful for you.

271

Introduce friends to other people you know who might enjoy their company as well.

272

Buy recycled products.

273

When dining at someone's home, thank the person who prepared the meal, comment on how good the food was, and offer to help clean the dishes.

274

Share your recipe with a guest who enjoyed a particular dish you prepared.

275

When you see a flashing 12 on the VCR machine of someone you know, offer to show them how to program it.

276

Prepare a warm bubble bath for your spouse at the end of the workday.

277

Give a loved one who has had a stressful day at work a massage.

278

Use coupons for products manufacturers advertise will benefit a non-profit organization. Sometimes companies donate a portion of the sales for a particular item to a charitable group.

279

When someone admires something of yours like a sweater or a vase, give it to them. If not, then tell them where you purchased it so they can get one for themselves.

280

Promote a non-profit organization you support every time you write a check by using Message!Check. The company incorporates a group's logo and/or message on every check and donates $1.00 with each order to the organization featured on the check.

Participating organizations - which include such groups as Mothers Against Drunk Driving and National Audubon Society - are detailed in a listing provided by Message!Check.

For more information, call Message!Check in Seattle, Washington at (800) 243-2565.

281

When at work, do your job so your co-workers won't have to do your job for you.

282

Take up a collection among those you work with to get a card and present for your boss on Bosses Day.

283

Take your medicine as directed.

284

Schedule annual check ups with your doctor. If you're a woman, make an appointment with your gynecologist to have a pap smear done once a year.

285

Attend a city council meeting to get a view of the important issues that are facing your community.

286

When a friend needs to have their car serviced, meet them at the car dealership and give them a ride home or to work. When the car is finished, give your friend a ride to the dealership to pick up the car.

287

Save someone's place in line who may need to step out for a quick moment.

288

While waiting for service, if someone comes to help you and you notice that another person has been waiting longer, let them know that the person who was there before you should be helped first.

289

Help a family in their efforts to find a missing child. Call the National Center for Missing and Exploited Children at (800) 843-5678 if you recognize a missing child featured in a flier or poster. The center can also put you in touch with the clearinghouse operation in your state that helps find missing children.

You can provide assistance simply by keeping on file the ADVO cards you receive in the mail with pictures of missing children and by referring to them when you suspect you've seen a featured child. Photo Partners hang up missing child posters in public places. If your business has a company newsletter, consider featuring a missing child in each issue.

290

When your new telephone directory books arrive, take your old books to a place that will recycle them. Contact your local litter prevention office for information on where the books may be recycled.

291

Arrange a going away party for an employee who is leaving your company. It sends a message to all employees that the company appreciates the work its employees have done. Have all employees sign a going away card with their own parting messages. Try to give the employee a gift that will remind them of your company such as a sweatshirt with your logo.

292

Keep an extra pair of sunglasses in your car. Offer the glasses to your front seat passenger if the sun is too bright.

293

Attempt to win a stuffed animal for your loved one at an amusement park or state fair.

294

Play bingo at your local church. It's a fun way to support your house of worship. If you win, use the money to do other good deeds.

295

Monitor the television programs your children watch. Use parental channel lock devices to limit the channels your children can have access to.

296

Donate a fan or air conditioner in the summer to the Salvation Army to give to a needy family.

297

When you finish eating your meal at a restaurant, stack your plates and place your silverware on top of the pile of dishes to make it easier for the bus person to clean your table.

298

~C~

Return your library books and tapes on time. Others may be waiting to check them out.

299

~C~

If you're good at speaking before groups, offer your services to a non-profit organization's speakers bureau. Speakers help the community become aware of the organization's services and needs.

300

Many organizations prepare free hot turkey meals to needy people on Thanksgiving and Christmas. If others in your household are preparing your meal, invite those in your family who aren't cooking to join you in helping serve food at the shelter for an hour or two.

301

Take your children to see the place where you grew up. Share stories about what life was like for you. Not only will it strengthen the family bond, but it will also give your children a stronger identity with family history.

302

Be true to your word. When you say you are going to do something and people are depending on you, do it. Don't make promises you can't keep.

303

If a Catholic friend of yours experiences a death in their family, arrange to have a mass said for the deceased person. This is usually scheduled around the anniversary of the death. Send the mass card to the family so they will know when the mass will be held.

304

Save newspaper and magazine articles you know someone would be interested in. Give or mail the articles to them promptly.

305

If you were taught by a nun, priest, or other religious person at a parochial school, show them your appreciation by contributing to the Retirement Fund for Religious. For more information write to:

Retirement Fund for Religious
P.O. Box 73140
Baltimore, MD 21273

306

Forgive others who may have wronged you.

307

Visit a sick friend. Ask if there is anything you can do to help such as prepare a meal or pick up a prescription.

308

Give your seat to another person if there aren't any seats left.

309

Many malls have food courts with dining areas. Often during lunch, it's hard to find an unoccupied table. If you have empty chairs at your table, invite others to sit with you to eat.

310

Call your local police department and arrange for an officer to speak with you and your neighbors about forming a neighborhood block watch program

311

Organize a block party with your neighbors in the summer. Have each family bring a covered dish. Plan entertainment for the children such as games, prizes, and a magic show.

312

Replace your car's headlight or break light when it burns out. Failure to do so inconveniences other motorists and may cause an accident.

313

Make a videotape of a person's family and friends talking about why that person is so special. This is a personal gift that can be given on someone's birthday. It's especially nice when given to someone who's moved a long distance away from home.

314

Ask those around you if it would bother them if you smoked before you do. Some people have trouble breathing when they're surrounded by smoke.

315

Admit when you've made a mistake. Don't try to place the blame with others or cover it up.

316

Compliment the way someone does their job while they're doing it.

317

Contact the director of a shelter for unwed pregnant teens. Hold a baby shower with your friends to benefit a teenage mother who's decided to keep her baby.

318

Buy a new toy and donate it to the U.S. Marine Corps Reserve's Toys for Tots program during the Christmas season. The toy must be unwrapped so it may be distributed to a child whose age and gender are appropriate for the gift.

319

Find out how your company can encourage its customers to donate to the Toys for Tots program. Offer customers a discount or free item if they donate a new toy through your company.

320

Use a credit card that benefits a non-profit organization every time you use it.

321

Speak respectfully to your parents at all times.

322

Call someone who's going through a difficult time in their life. Ask them how they're doing and just listen.

323

When a store offers a "buy one get one free" promotion, give the free item to a non-profit organization that distributes materials to the needy.

324

Go fishing with your children and give away some of what you catch.

325

Find out if your local library has a storybook reading time for children. If so, offer to read a book.

326

Have your business give its customers an unexpected gift during the Christmas gift-giving season. A local gas station gave customers who filled their tanks a coaster with a beautiful painting of Santa Claus laminated on the top. An eye doctor gave children aged 12 and under a coupon for a free scoop of ice cream at a family restaurant near his office.

Think of a creative, inexpensive way you can surprise your customers with a feeling of joy.

327

Spend at least five minutes in the morning in quiet meditation or in prayer. Reflect on how you can help others as you begin your day. If it's hard for you to find the time to do this, do it while you're in the shower or on your commute to work.

328

Donate baked goods to a club or organization's bake sale.

329

Give supportive information to someone who's interested in pursuing the same career as you. People learn to be successful in a given field by modeling those who are already successful in their accomplishments.

330

When meeting someone new, always offer your hand in a handshake.

331

Offer to help pay for the gas when you travel a long distance by car with someone.

332

Purchase gift certificates from a barber or hair salon and give them to people in the welfare office, on the unemployment line, or at a homeless shelter. You may also have an agency that serves the underprivileged distribute them.

333

Write for tickets to popular national television shows. When you receive the tickets, go to a travel agency and ask that the agents offer them to customers who will be in the city at the time of the taping.

Tickets to national television shows are free. Find out from your local network affiliate that carries the program where you should write for tickets.

334

See how your business can help a non-profit organization by donating services or offering them at a reduced rate. Some examples of how this has been done: Doctors gave free physical exams to a parochial school's football team. A computer training company donated 50 class seats to the local United Way. A printing company printed a group's schedule of activities.

If your business helps the community, people perceive it as caring and viable. Your employees will feel the same and have a sense of pride about where they work.

335

Find out what your gift is and use it to help others. If you're good at sewing, make clothes for underprivileged children. If you're good at playing a musical instrument, play one night at a nursing home. If you enjoy talking on the phone, call a friend you may have lost touch with. The more you use a gift for the benefit of others, the better you become at it.

336

When you see that someone needs emergency help, get involved by calling the proper authorities. If someone's physically hurt, call an ambulance. If a crime is taking place, call the police. If you suspect child abuse, call the children's services office.

337

Visit a religious service that is different from your own. You'll have a better understanding and respect for different faiths.

338

Help entertain a bored or restless child on a long flight by paying for the movie earphone rental. Show the flight attendant which child you'd like to surprise. Make it an anonymous gift.

339

If you don't own a U.S. flag, buy one.

340

Fly the U.S. flag outside your home or office on Memorial Day, Veterans Day, and the Fourth of July. Veterans and the families of those who gave their lives for their country will be touched knowing their sacrifices are appreciated by their fellow citizens.

341

Have a grocery store deliver fruit baskets to your local police and fire departments thanking them for their services.

342

Reupholster old furniture and donate it to the Salvation Army to give to families whose homes have been destroyed by fire.

343

Invest in your employees. Pay for them to attend seminars, workshops, and classes that will improve their skills and performance at work.

344

Notice things to genuinely compliment another person's appearance and do so. While appearances aren't everything, we all feel a little better when someone says we look good.

345

Excess food at restaurants, hotels, and bake shops can be used to feed the hungry. Many communities have a program in which volunteers pick up and deliver food to drop off sites.

Find out if your area has such a program, and see if there's a route which is on your way home from work. If so, offer to transport the food at your convenience.

346

Vote in every election.

347

Volunteer to work on the election campaign of a candidate or issue you support. You can help by stuffing envelopes, answering phones, or putting up signs.

348

Learn the facts about AIDS. Call (800) 342-AIDS (2437) for more information.

349

Buy a compact disc or cassette tape of music that puts you in a good mood. Play it whenever you need to lift your spirits.

350

Don't waste food. Take only what you can eat.

351

Place a bumper sticker on your vehicle that has an uplifting, positive message. You may never know how many worried, sad, or preoccupied motorists will find encouragement in your message of good cheer.

352

Take an ornament from a Giving Tree during the Christmas season and buy an appropriate gift for the person chosen. You can find Giving Trees in churches, businesses, malls, and some community service agencies.

An ornament may have "Boy age 6" written on it. The person who selects it should then buy and wrap an appropriate present and tape the ornament on the gift for distribution. Check how your local Giving Tree program operates since procedures may vary. Giving Trees are designed to provide presents for underprivileged children and nursing home residents.

353

When visiting out of town friends or relatives, give them something your area is known for. If you're from Maine, bring live lobsters. If you're from Florida, bring a box of oranges.

354

Some mail carriers must walk on their routes, and in the summer it can be physically draining. If you notice your mail carrier is hot, sweating, and out of breath, offer them a glass of ice water and a cold wash cloth to wipe their face.

355

Send a "Thinking of You" card to a friend you haven't kept in very good touch with over the years.

356

Have your company sponsor a field trip to a nearby zoo or museum for a class at an elementary school.

357

Contribute to a private or parochial school's scholarship fund so an underprivileged child may be given the opportunity to attend such a school.

358

Find out how many inmates are at your local jail. Send enough Christmas cards to the facility so that each inmate will receive one. Include a general hand written message in each card. This act may be done anonymously if you so desire.

359

Enroll in a self-defense class. It will give you the skills and confidence to help you get out of a dangerous situation.

360

Rewind video and audio cassette tapes before returning them to the library or video store.

361

Have your business sponsor an award at a local school for a student who has shown dedication to community service. The award could be a certificate, plaque, trophy, or savings bond.

362

Have your child participate in a finger-printing program. Some schools and businesses sponsor a program in which children have their photographs and fingerprints taken. Parents keep the information to help authorities locate or identify their children in the event they are missing.

363

Instead of bagging your groceries in a plastic or paper bag, bring your own reusable canvas bag.

364

If you use the plastic bags your grocer gives you, bring them to the store the next time you shop. Many grocery stores have a bin at the store's entrance for you to drop off your used plastic bags. Your grocer will then send them out to be recycled.

365

Reduce the amount of junk mail that's sent to you. Call businesses and organizations that send you unwanted mail and ask them to stop sending you their material. To keep your name from being placed on junk mailing lists, write to the Mail Preference Service, Direct Marketing Association, P.O. Box 9008, Farmingdale, NY 11735. You should notice a reduction in junk mail within 90 days.

366

Instead of using disposable cups at work, keep a coffee mug in your office desk to use whenever you want a drink. It will help to reduce the amount of landfill waste.

367

Rather than writing a letter, try taping your message on an audio cassette and mail it to your loved ones. This is an ideal and inexpensive keepsake for grandparents who enjoy hearing their grandchild's voice.

368

Take the time to hear yourself laugh. Watch a funny movie that will make your sides ache.

369

Buy playground toys for children at your local elementary school. Some of the relatively inexpensive items you may consider donating include jump ropes, kick balls, and basketballs.

370

Read to the blind in your area. Some communities have a radio reading service program for the blind in which visually impaired people are supplied with a special radio that picks up local programs for the blind.

Volunteers read and record on tape sections of a newspaper or magazine which is later broadcasted. Call your local United Way office for information on organizations that serve the blind in your neighborhood.

371

Begin an exercise program for yourself under your doctor's supervision. Do something everyday aimed at improving your physical fitness. You could take a walk on your lunch break, buy an exercise video, or join a health club.

372

Clip coupons and mail them to area shelters for the needy. Some organizations make coupons available for those in need of financial assistance to choose from. Call the shelter first to see if the coupons would be helpful.

373

Save Heinz baby food or juice labels and give them to a children's hospital near you. Heinz Baby Food Label-Saving Program will donate up to 6 cents to participating hospitals for each label collected.

The money is used to purchase toys, games, patient care equipment, and other items for children. Thousands of dollars are awarded to hospitals every year. Call Heinz Baby Food in Pittsburgh, Pennsylvania for the location of a participating children's hospital in your area at (800) USA-BABY (872-2229).

374

Raise a puppy that will later become a service dog for a person with visual or hearing disabilities. Puppy raisers give love, care, and nurturing to animals before they're old enough to go through their specialized training. Various organizations provide puppy raisers with a seven to nine week old puppy which is raised in their home for about one year.

Labrador Retrievers, German Shepherds, and Golden Retrievers are the most common breeds used for service dog training. The Delta Society can refer you to an organization in your area that has a puppy raiser program. For more information, call (800) 869-6898.

375

Give a teddy bear to someone who needs comfort or companionship. Good Bears of the World (GBW) is an international non-profit organization that receives requests for bears from hospitals, police departments, nursing homes, and others who want to help those in need such as a traumatized child who has witnessed the death of a loved one in a car accident or an elderly person in a nursing home who has no one to visit them.

GBW has created a Bear Bank to supply bears for those who request them. Your small contribution can assist GBW. If you would like to request or order a bear, make a donation to the Bear Bank, or receive more information about the organization, call the GBW headquarters in Toledo, Ohio at (419) 531-5365.

376

Set aside a certain amount of money from each paycheck to do good things for others. This will make it easier for you to spend the money on good deeds rather than on personal desires since you'll already have the money budgeted out. You may even consider opening a separate savings or checking account for your philanthropic works.

377

Let love be the fragrance you leave behind wherever you go. Don't waste an opportunity to show someone your love. Review the previous pages and select one suggestion to do *immediately* upon completing this book.

Dear Reader,

Thank you for purchasing this book. We hope you found the information useful and will tell your friends about it. If you have other suggestions on how busy people can make a difference, please share them with us. Your ideas may be compiled in another book to inspire others.

Also, we'd like to know what kind of an impact doing the good things in this book has had on you and the people you've helped. Please include your name, address, and phone number with your correspondence. Mail your suggestions or comments to:

Helping Hand Publishers
P.O. Box 58673
Cincinnati, OH 45258

About the Author

Marie Angnardo is a researcher/writer/speaker who consults with businesses who want to have a positive impact on their community. She spent several years working as News/Public Affairs Director at WNCD-FM in Youngstown, Ohio where she met regularly with community leaders to ascertain the needs and interests of the surrounding areas. In addition to writing and producing public service announcements for radio and television, she also coordinated special events to benefit non-profit organizations. She graduated from Fordham University in New York City with a degree in English and currently resides in Cincinnati, Ohio.